Manuel José de la Candelaria Mier y Ponte

Matanzas, Cuba

THE SHARK IN THE DINING ROOM

MIER PONTE

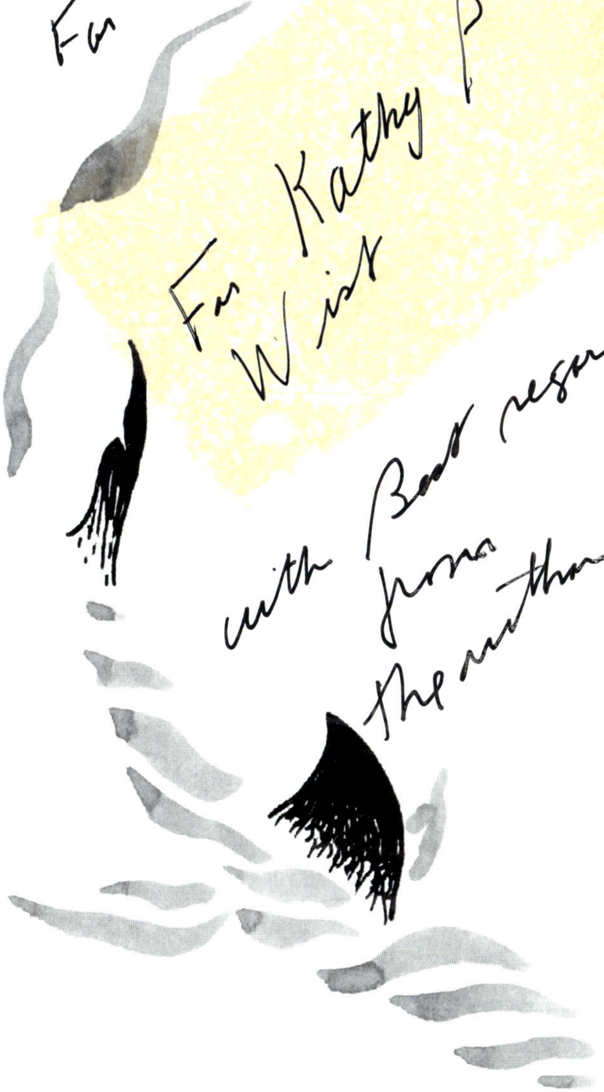

HEAVENLY WIND PRESS

Published by Heavenly Wind Press
P.O. Box 631
Selma, Oregon 97538
For promotional or order information only, please call:
Telephone: (541) 597-2866

Cover illustration by Curtis Bloom.
Cover design and electronic production by Rose-Merkle Design.
Edited by Jonah Bornstein, Mier Ponte and Chris Rose-Merkle.
Printed in the United States of America by Mustard Press, Inc.

Library of Congress Catalog Card Number: 95-81155
ISBN: 0-9649763-0-7

This work is dedicated to all those who hate their
tormentors.

To the Neighbors of the North:
"...they all grew drowsy, and fell asleep."
      — (Matthew XXV, 5 KV)

and...

To the Islanders:
*"When the sixth hour came, there was darkness over all the
earth until the ninth hour; and at the ninth hour Jesus cried
out with a loud voice,..."My God, my God, why hast thou
forsaken me?"*
      — (Mark XV, 33-34, KV)

Acknowledgements

It should be obvious from the book how much this is the work of my father, Dr. Casto Mier Zurbano, also known as Casto Mier, who appointed me as his literary executor. Furthermore, he named me custodian of photographic material, as well as of the legacy of doing things "the Mier way".

The completion of the book is primarily due to the always patient and sustained support of Chris Rose-Merkle, who did not limit his assistance to the graphic design of the project, but also played a significant role as an artist, advisor and, at times, supportive psychotherapist.

Kathy Mustard and Pete L'Ivers supplied the guidance through the complex process of printing and electronic reproduction of photographic material. For this I am very grateful.

Curtis Bloom devoted much effort to the art rendition of the title.

Agnes Hughes typed with excellence the original manuscript, and provided much needed inspirational stimulus.

I owe words of encouragement and insight to Evelyn Mier, who saw the first version of "A Story Without Faces".

Finally, I am indebted to Diana Mier, my wife, who has foregone so much so I may devote time and thought to *The Shark in the Dining Room*.

*One day Irving explained about the sharks to Peter. "Sharks
are animals who seem very tame and nice; but finally, in a
treacherous way, they come near you and eat you up." After
that, Peter's feelings for Irving changed.*

— Silvano Arieti, *Interpretation of Schizophrenia*

*"But, I am not guilty," said K., "It's a misunderstanding.
And, if it comes to that, how can any man be called guilty?
We are all simply men here, one as much as the other."*

*"That is true," said the priest, "but that's how all guilty men
talk."*

— Franz Kafka, *The Trial.*

A STORY WITHOUT FACES

THE COLONEL'S CUFF

The sunlight abruptly hit the dirty glass of the only window in the room and awakened him. With slow and deliberate movements, he left the bed and stood naked in the center of the small room. Once again, he understood the meaning of the title of a novel his daughter once told him about, *Bonjour Tristesse*. Prior to the day when the big push of the "glori ous revolution" ended in his imprisonment, all words of despair, were remote to him. Up to that time, life with its demands and its complexities, was always reduced by his methodic mind to a job that had to be done. He walked slowly to the window, his hand passing in a mechanical gesture over his once neatly trimmed mustache. The window, close to the ceiling,forced him to look upwards. He muttered in a whisper a "Hail Mary." This, he had done for more than forty years, ever since he was a youngster in the strict catholic school only a few blocks away from the prison. The itching of the growing beard, a vague smell of old urine in the room and the stale taste in his mouth induced the anguish, hopelessness and despair that he experienced each morning. Against his will, he became aware that he had not taken a bath since his arrest. Perhaps this could account for his state of solitude and anxiety, with the awareness of approaching death, the only certain knowledge. He resisted this tendency to link the objective phenomena of running water over his body to his subjective experience.

The face of his assistant, a major he met in the long war with the rebels, appeared in his mind. "Sir!," the face barked, "you are cracking up." He shivered and took an empty wooden box, which he used as a chair, and moved it close to the window. He stood on it, bringing his face almost to the window, with the hope that some of the clean morning air would filter through a crack of the glass. With his long, lean body, he resembled, under the sun, an exotic bird in his cage. His nakedness became more apparent as the room flooded with light; as a stage at the beginning of a play. Behind his nakedness, he thought, lay the secret of his entire life.

During the process of admission to the prison, he was ordered to remove his clothes. He surrendered his neat, crisp khaki uniform with the same sadness and reverence defeated old soldiers surrendered their swords. He waited, embarrassed, in his underwear, for hours, and was finally given a crude uniform made of the cheapest denim. He had worn that uniform for several days while the process of daily questioning admixed with threats and insults was going on. He was not beaten, because he was one of the most important cards in the skilled hands of the hero of the revolution. And now, today, he was to appear in public in front of the revolutionary court, which in a few hours would decide his fate. Because of this, he had given his rumpled uniform to his wife the night before, when, in an unusual gesture of kindness from the heroes of the revolution, she was allowed to visit him for a few minutes.

A number of confusing noises began to crowd in the cell. Many were coming from the central patio where the rebel troops were drilling. He looked at them through the dirty window. Looking and listening to them, it occurred to him that every group of people has its own brand of feelings which is projected in the way its members dress and in the way they talk. The latter being only the consequence of the former. The troops were dressed in the most varied uniforms; the head gear exhibiting the greatest diversity. Some wore green, red or black berets; whereas others had hats made of fiber ranging from the small, almost ridiculous size of the western part of the country to the big wide-brimmed Texan style. There was a sprinkling of a few regular army caps of assorted colors. Bearded faces and bright handkerchiefs around the neck were not uncommon. The variety of color and textures, coupled with the disorder in formation gave the appearance of a well rehearsed musical show rather than a routine military drill. The lieutenant in charge gave all orders in grunts, which seldom reached the articulation of speech.

The overall impression was for him vaguely familiar and appeared as an exaggeration of his son's behavior at the time when he used such words as "ontology," "encounter," "course of life" and "existentialism." Rapidly approaching steps were heard beyond the door and when they ceased, the lock screamed, as if being tortured by the key. His wife stood for a moment in the darkness of the hall flanked by two rebel officers. Without looking at him, she rapidly crossed the room to the bed, placed a bundle on the naked mattress, and said "Here." He liked her apparent lack of emotion in front of the officers. She had never been too articulate, but since his arrest, she hardly ever spoke. The overwhelming change, unlike what it had done to other women, had silenced her. She stood by the bed with her hands held in tight fists but without emotion in her pale face. He opened the neatly wrapped package and was pleasantly surprised by the pressed uniform. The denim with the heavy starch had developed a stiff and dense consistency and, due to the pressing, was shiny like a cheap plastic. He unfolded the trousers and was amazed and delighted to see that, with careful pressing, she had devised cuffs in them. They had been too long, and he had been disturbed by the feeling of his pants dragging on the floor whenever he walked to the office of the G-2 to be questioned. He turned to see her face of delight, and in a moment she was gone.

He was, once again, alone. He dressed rapidly. The rasping noise of the lock once again announced a new visitor. This time, there were many officers and soldiers, if the rebels could be called that, he thought. He was concerned by the sudden deference that all showed him. Once more, against his will, the thought that his physical appearance caused the change, entered his mind. In silence he left the cell, joining the group in the dark corridor. As he was walking with these men, he thought of himself, as he always did, as a leader. Soon they were close to the amphitheater where the rapid, yet lethal, sessions of the military courts were being held. As he walked, he felt grateful to his wife for having given him the only weapon that she could in a moment like this. Close to the main door of the courtroom there was a large mirror. He could not resist the vanity and he walked slowly towards it. Trying to appear casual, he stood in front of the mirror and looked at himself. He felt ashamed and cheated. The uncombed hair, the growing beard, the tired expression in his face gave his shiny and starched prison uniform a fake appearance. Had he arrived at the end of what he thought had been a perfect life? Was everything to be destroyed not only outside but also inside of himself? To exaggerate the awareness of his humanity he felt like moving his bowels, which he had not done for three days. He had a sudden urge to look at his dirty shoes and to keep his face down. His name was called in a loud voice from inside the courtroom. His last name was mispronounced. And he felt angry. Cannibals, he thought. Anthropoids and cannibals, he thought. And the overwhelming anger made his body erect and vibrant.

As he entered the room, the crowd produced a muffled sound, which reminded him of the sea at low tide. He walked to the front row of seats as if he was marching in a victorious military parade. As he approached the seats, reserved for the accused, a few scattered insults, emitted in low voices, began to flow from the crowd. These small cries were so separated that they reminded him of the sick yellow flowers he had seen growing in many heavily scarred battlefields. The words began to grow in intensity and number, and as they grew, they be came bolder and filthier. He stopped and turned around to face the audience. Rapidly all voices died, and for a few moments, he could only hear the movement of their sweaty bodies rubbing the benches. A stench of fear was coming from the crowd. He had smelled frightened crowds before, but in none, had their rancid scent been so putrid. Vaguely he could hear his name being called again, and this familiar sound was followed immediately by the monotonous enumeration of all his war crimes. Strangely enough, the diction seemed to belong to a well educated person. He looked at him and recognized that the prosecutor was a well known professor of law. The colonel studied, with attention, the gesticulating figure. There was a disproportion between his moving limbs and the monotone of his voice. The dark mustache seemed to be one piece with the heavy frames of the eyeglasses. The drops of sweat in the never ending forehead looked artificial because they did not move or fall even at the time of his most eloquent gyrations. He stopped paying attention to the leonine face and was amazed to find that the inflections in his voice were in accordance with his education but, above all, appropriate to the situation. He did not search for words. He knew it all. In the same manner that physicians and judges can boil down all the ills of humans with the statement that they had seen a "similar case" before. He tended to repeat himself whenever he made use of a well known slogan of the revolution. Whenever burping one of such common-place phrases, he stammered a little. The stammering in combination with the flat tone of the voice gave an impression of having been rehearsed. For a moment, the colonel pictured in his mind the magnificent professor of law rehearsing the slogans of the revolution, alone, in his room, in front of a mirror. A smile began to grow out of the corner of the colonel's mouth. It failed to bloom into laughter because when paying attention to the words, he recognized a monstrosity. This man who once had been the chairman of the department of penal law in the National University was stating the need to make the laws retroactive in nature. He heard vaguely the last sentence where the professor stated that "our new laws must provide punishment for crimes committed in the present or the future, but also must learn to sink their claws into the past." The colonel had expected that if executed, he would have had the comfort of having been illegally killed. But, if the revolutionary government had already made the penal code of retroactive nature, his death would be in accordance with the law. This meant to regress historically 200 years before the era of Beccaria. Therefore, his execution would be "legal." Despair struck him. He felt no fear or anger but only an intense somnolence. His eyes almost closed and he felt a surging desire to yawn. He tried to repress or swallow the uncontrollable movements of his chest and throat but gave in. After his big yawn a tear rested in the corner of his right eye.

Then, the procession began. To the colonel, it gave the impression that it was an unending repetition of the same human being. It is true that the height, weight, color of hair and facial expressions changed slightly from one to the other. Yet, they all had the same rudimentary diction, the same voice inflections, the same tone of slighted dignity in their voices. And all were asked the same question, "Do you recognize in this room, the person who tortured and killed the people in your town?" Some of them answered with words, most however, raised their right index finger and hesitatingly pointed two or three times towards the colonel. None of them looked, their eyes wandering aimlessly at the crowd. After their brief performance each one would again be swallowed by the gray mass. All the men behaved the same. They all walked to the witness stand slowly, heads down and when returning to their seats, rushed with outstretched hands as if demanding recognition. The few women who followed were quite different. They walked quickly and soberly along. As the question was asked of them, a crackle of high-pitched laughter erupted from the blushing faces. Still the same accusing right index finger was raised and pointed at the colonel. He was beginning to feel as conspicuous as he indeed was. With the well pressed uniform shiny in the morning sun, he knew that all eyes explored him. They had been waiting. They were still waiting and perhaps they would never see the sign of weakness, which represented for them the complete victory of the revolution. He remembered the words of the man in charge of his questioning at the G-2. He had said "We are going to break you." And after a pause, he added; "Quickly." But so far the colonel had been so able to detach himself from what was happening that no one could ever have said that he had submitted.

The repetitious nature of the scene at the witness stand began to bore him. He studied the three men sitting high who represented the judges. There was no difference between them and the faces in the crowd The presiding figure, in the center, was dozing. His tranquility only broke when he made almost comical facial contortions and clumsy movements with his right arm to keep a fly away from his nostrils. The man, on the right, was drinking beer straight from the bottle, and after each big swallow, he would wipe his mouth with the sleeve of his shirt. He seemed to have a generous provision of the yellow liquid under the table. As soon as one bottle was empty, he would produce, almost like magic, a new full one. His eyes converged on the bottle each time he elevated the elbow above the table as if afflicted with a severe case of squint. The man to the left, was thin. He looked almost mysterious behind the enormous dark green sun glasses. He sat erect and seemed to be the only one really attentive to the statements of the witnesses. Occasionally, he would write notes in a copy book. His interest and application appeared so unusual and such a contrast with the others that the colonel knew he was the man sent to make sure that things would go according to what was planned beforehand by the head of the revolution. He was like the assistant director and producer. The one to make sure that the drama, written step by step by the brain and the heart of the movement, would be entertaining and above all "truthful." The thin man was a pawn. A big pawn with dark glasses, but nothing but a pawn. He, the colonel thought, must conceal that he is hollow and would not dare to look at the man, who would soon, wearing his denim uniform, face a firing squad.

Who was behind all of his power? Who was playing skillfully, one piece against another to the incalculable advantage of himself? Who had created an opposition of morals between generations to move the younger people against the older? The last words of a sentence, coming from the prosecutor gave the answer "the head of the revolution." Who was this monster of stone? Where did he hide? Who was that man anyway? Where did he come from? The title of "head of the revolution" did not fit him well. In spite of his marvelous, often-called Christ-like head.

He thought of the phrase, often used by his mother when she went crazy. She had gone to a private sanitarium where she continued to repeat like a prayer the monks whispered in the evenings: "I have a shark in the dining room." According to the psychiatrist who worked with her for several days, she was trying to say that she had a cancer of the stomach. However, she was so fearful of cancer, especially in the stomach, that she would not even dare to pronounce, to verbalize, or to place on her lips the horrible words. This was almost identical, he thought, to the way the neighbors of the North were dealing with the problem of the purulent island. Yet, the sickness of the island and the sickness of the neighbors was the same. The neighbors up North appeared to be strong and healthy and full of life and strength. The men always so well tanned and, above all, they had beautiful, well taken care of teeth. Yet, they were so fearful that the accusation of the hero of the revolution, that the Northerners were all weak, seemed to be true. He had even accused the handsome, almost beautiful president of that country of being a "pansy." And, the president had answered saying something like "the representation of the party of the first part...etc," which meant nothing to him or to anybody. The colonel began to wonder if he could suggest to the president to use a more appropriate name. Perhaps, he could say, "The representation of the shark in the dining room is incorrect." And all the psychiatrists and perhaps even more, all the physicians, and perhaps all people would know what he was talking about.

Yes, the island had once been the main source of all the sugar cane that the country of the North consumed. It was also an important source of coffee and tobacco. And, when the fellows from the North felt like getting rid of the cold in their white strong bones, they came to the island, to bask in the sun, to see a good show and both men and women would come to get satisfying, easy to get, and above all inexpensive, sex. Well, isn't that a good description of a dining room? Yes, he would suggest to the president of the country of the North to use that title. Those words perhaps would not scare them as much, but they would be easier to pronounce than "the party of the first part" bit and it would be a more accurate portrayal of the man that was going to execute him.

For a moment the colonel stared at the picture, the only picture, which hung in the room. It was dusty and askew. Yet, under it, some hands had placed a few paper flowers, held against the crumbling plaster with black tape. The flowers did not contradict the painting. In it, was "the hero," holding in one hand his telescopic-sighted rifle and in the other, a small child with a rotten smile. The myopic and black eyes of "the hero" were staring back at him. He wondered if they were accusing him, the colonel, of being the shark in the dining room. Whoever proved to be the stronger would get the title, like in a boxing match, or in a chess game.

He understood that there was more at stake than a pressed uniform or a personification. The colonel's attitude and gestures, if strong enough, could make an idea survive forever, even though his body would be buried under a handful of earth. Or of cow dung. By the way things were going in the trial, it was easy to see that there was a big effort behind the colonel's court appearance. Each witness, each report, even each grunt emitted by one of the members of the stinking crowd added ammunition to the almost compulsory guilty sentence.

And the revolution was economical. Like all underdogs are. It was obvious then, that the big effort was aimed at something more than just to kill a man. His eyes drifted down once more to his neatly pressed uniform. It was at this moment his only support, his only comfort, his only weapon. Seen from a distance, he knew it would be as impressive as a tree. Trees appear perfect from a distance. Yet, you can see all the cracks and rot in their bark when you look close. You can also see the insects crawling on the surface and worms burrowing and searching. That is the way the material covering his right knee looked. In spite of the starch, there were myriads of small button-shaped protrusions, as if the clothing had developed a severe case of contagious warts. In a vain effort, he tried to erase them with his thumb. He even tried, after observing whether too many eyes were watching him, to use some saliva from his lips to flatten them out. It was of no use. While in the middle of this operation, the silence from the crowd startled the colonel and he looked up to the table where the three members of the martial court were seated. The secretary, with a decided gesture, placed his bottle out of the vision of the audience and stood up. He did not dare to push his chair out of the way because of the narrowness of the podium. In an almost crouched position, the physical discomfort showing in his flat and monotone voice, he stated: "The prisoner is to come forward to hear the verdict of the court."

The colonel stood up and moved towards the center of the room. At this time, the entire gray mass began to howl and scream. The colonel turned around and was amazed to see that all of the members of the audience had the same posture. Mouths wide open, eyes flashing, the veins of the face and neck distended and the right arm raised with the fist closed as if holding an object. Even the children were holding their right arm up with an angry gesture. He could not understand the meaning of the extended right arm. Was it, perhaps, some form of salutation? for him? for the court? It soon became apparent to him what it meant when, in a disorganized manner, hundreds of varied projectiles began to hit him. Tomatoes, rotten eggs, pieces of lettuce and even stones began to stream from the crowd towards him. Being in the center of the room there was no danger of making the members of the court a target. He turned to face the court again to see that the president, removed from his protracted somnolence, was laughing noisily as he was applauding. The noise continued until the secretary, using his handgun as a mallet, called the populace to order.

When the colonel approached the court, the president in an involuntary gesture stood up. Embarrassed, he sat down rapidly and muttered, "The prisoner is found guilty of all charges and sentenced to death." After a pause he added, "Does the prisoner have any statement to make?" He had not expected this opportunity. The entire court proceeding had resembled more the "local color" of a Roman circus, rather than the ethical attitude of a court of law. His delight was soon over. After the last word from the president of the court, the screaming began again. This time an obvious effort for over-achievement was on every lip and in every throat. He had to scream his defiance and rebellion at the evil which had unleashed forces that some day, man could no longer contain. But how? Rapidly, he thought, I must do it rapidly. If not, it will be one more defeat. His mind looked back into everything he knew. How did Caesar send the fallen gladiator to death? He knew. By showing his hand with the thumb pointing to the ground. This is practically what had been done to the colonel. To answer the death sentence with a hand sign, that was meaningful enough, to be understood by a crowd of peasants and cannibals was a challenge. The colonel turned towards the crowd and said, "I have a statement to make." His words were lost in the howling of the crowd. He raised his middle finger like the mast of a banner. The high-pitched laughter of the children in the front row, followed by the sudden silence which fell upon the room, showed him that they, all of them, understood.

The return to the cell was a let-down, after his brief moment of glory. Somewhere along the cavernous hall of the old prison, it occurred to him that, in the past, going there was his usual excuse to the wife, to spend a free afternoon with his mistress. The Fortress having been, for years, an exclusive club or meeting place for the few officers of higher ranks and their guests. He listened and in his mind heard the tune which his empty-headed but attractive girlfriend used to hum. But, it was not imaginary music he was hearing. A loud speaker or a distant radio blew the tropical rhythm to him on the afternoon breeze. The colonel had another brief, yet intense feeling of despair. The distant and quiet little noise made him think of old times. He could not picture his mistress' full and feminine body but he could almost hear her — as when making love to him, she would pause for a moment and leering towards him, would say, "You like that, eh?"

The heavy and dark metallic door in front of him brought him back. As he entered the room, he could not help but notice a blue envelope resting on top of the only piece of furniture in the room. The empty wooden box. He pretended surprise. He approached the object and held it in his hand. A soft fragrance and the familiar handwriting brought with it a thought of her. He turned his face towards the guard asking a useless question, "What is this?" With apparent deference, he gave a most unusual answer, "Knowing you will soon be dead, our beloved hero wanted you to have a final word from your favorite bitch." The thoughtfulness of the colonel's enemies was an element of comfort.

He heard the heavy door closing. Once again alone. He opened the letter slowly, fearful of an unwanted surprise. The neat handwriting took hold of his attention. He read and reread the message again. He saw it and was unbelieving. Yet, the stark obscenity of his mistress message was too clear to be ignored. The events described on the little blue stationary read like a cheap pornographic story. In an attempt to intercede for the colonel and save his life, she had gone to see the head of the Revolution. She visited him, in his main office at the Naval War Department. While there and while alone with the tall, bearded figure and while pleading for the life of the colonel, felt an intense desire to be possessed by this man. She thought that, perhaps, this would even help her plea. She was capable of expressing her thoughts aloud. His answer was very plain, "If you want to have sex with me, you may, but I am in a hurry." He proceeded to remove her underclothes and without removing his own, had perfunctory sex with her while she was lying on her back on the big table at the Naval Department. The colonel's favorite woman had been thus agreeably raped. He wondered what she felt or what she thought while betraying him. He just wondered. He felt the information enter his consciousness. Little else, neither pleasure nor pain. He closed his eyes and in a tired gesture threw the letter to the floor. He could have gone sideways in his thinking. Yet, a stubborn fragment of his feelings kept on drawing all his attention to questions. Had he learned any thing? Had she learned anything? He could not answer for her, but he himself knew that all these events had brought him in painful, almost exasperating contact with reality. Reality? What is that?, he thought. He looked at the corner of the cell where the crumpled letter waited for him. A human being had taken that piece of blue paper, made by the hand of man and with an instrument, also made by the hand of man, had created a number of signs carrying to its destination, intended intense pain. Until the moment he became aware of the humanity of his mistress, he felt he could take anything. Even at the time of the initial fear of the detention, he had found a safe refuge in the memory of her and now it was all gone. There was a time when anything coming from her was sacred to him. A tear from her eyes was as sacred as the small, whitish stain in the seat of her panties. The thought of her lying on her back on a heavy mahogany desk on the 17th floor of the Naval War Department had thrown him out of his secure and, until recently, happy earthly medium. And, all of this, my God, he thought, willingly. If she would have been killed, the pain would, he knew, become a part of his being but her apparent transfiguration was for the colonel a force that meant a translation to another sphere. To his objective and methodical mind, it was a mystery that it had taken not guns, explosions, or fire, but a little piece of blue paper to have him suddenly distorted, avulsed and misplaced in the old, well known, solid world. He wondered if his anguish was the same, no more and no less, as Adam's when thrown out of the Garden of Eden. Perhaps, he thought, Adam read, "at the breezy time of the day," a little note from Eve, informing him that she had been, for some time, fornicating with the serpent. The face of the major again crept in his mind. He expected that it would spit, once more, the well known "cracking up" tune. It did not. This time, in a controlled voice, the face said, "Sir, we can not expect positive results from negative influences." Was he indeed right? Had the colonel, unknowingly, so corrupted the girl to a point where a sense of loyalty could not survive? The walls of the cell began to waver as the sense of guilt grew.

He closed his eyes tightly and stood quiet and motionless. Each time he opened his eyes the gray walls swam incessantly. All of these physical manifestations distracted his trend of thought and for a moment, willfully, he centered all his attention on them. Clearly, he remembered having felt this way once, only once. The first time he had been exposed to enemy fire. He walked to the wooden box and sat with a big effort. He opened his eyes slowly and with an uncontrollable movement vomited between his legs. Then, he began to retch, noisily. When he opened his eyes again, he saw in front of him a pair of dirty boots. His eyes moved with effort to the pants, the belt, the jacket and finally the face of the guard. He had entered without the colonel's awareness. His attitude looked almost hopeful as he asked, "Sir, are you ill?" With a nasal voice, from the vomitus in his nostrils, the colonel answered, "Nothing of importance, probably something I ate."

In silence, he went to the naked mattress in the corner of the room and dropped himself on it. And he sighed. As he closed his eyes, multiple visions began to torture his mind. He saw himself running in a wide open field. As he was running, a sense of unreality became so concrete and thick, he could touch it. Nothing has occurred, he thought. He forgot for a moment that he had been found guilty and was condemned to die. Found solace in the thought, "how nice it would be to return acquitted from the trial or to escape." What for? to emigrate to the North. He said in his cell in a loud voice, "I want to go to the North." The conviction in his voice died as suddenly as he began his utterance. What for? To fight for the rest of his life in a foreign environment and to be unable to live ever again in Paradise. Then he thought, there are many other places to go. Yet, he had in his youth travelled enough to realize that only the island was Paradise. Eden. And from his bible studies a voice became apparent. "And from the ground, the Lord God caused to grow every tree that was pleasing to the sight and good for food." Yet, he also knew what else had happened there. On one bright day Eve left a note for Adam and informed him of her affair with a Serpent and that was the end. This, after the Lord had said, "It is not good for man to be alone, I will make a fitting helper for him." Obviously this time, the Lord had been of no help. As he had many times in his army tent in the jungle, the colonel experienced a soft, sad, warm feeling and cried. Then he fell asleep.

It was still dark when the noises from the corridor awakened him. The rasping sound of the lock announced a visitor. The noise was accompanied by a reaction of his body which he could not control. He felt, without fear, some of his body hair standing on his back and an intense desire to swallow. His reaction, now he knew, was identical to what he felt when a teacher would scrape a blackboard covered with chalk dust with her fingernail. Or when a child would rub a Coke cap or an empty can against a sidewalk. Immersed in these thoughts and lying on his side facing the wall, he did not notice the entrance of the guard in the cell. The guard coughed respectfully and then in a low voice said, "Sir," it is time..." Without looking at him, he felt a violent repulsion and nausea. This guard, whose physical appearance was quite different from the others was the cause, he thought. The poor fellow was always neatly shaven and had the fair skin of those descendants of Italians or Northern Spaniards who never tanned in spite of the burning sun. He always appeared to the colonel as the living reproduction of Giovanni Arnolfini, in the famous painting by Jan Van Eyck. And he thought of Giovanni transported out of his century and out of his painting and out of his marriage to Giovanna Cenami and into this island with the bright skies and luminous sun. What for? Not to tan but to get sunburned and peel. And then get sunburned again. And peel again. Giovanni Arnolfini peeling his skin again and again, endlessly. The face of the major crept again into his mind and once more barked, "Sir, you are cracking up." The respectful voice again croaked, this time with a questioning tone, "Sir...?" He turned around and without leaving the bed looked at the guard. He had the apologetic posture that the peasants assume in front of superiors. Both hands held in front of the chest, with woven fingers, the trunk inclined forwards and the eyes looking to the sides, without looking into the colonel's eyes. The posture heightened the nausea, and in a defensive gesture, the colonel stood up, naked in the center of the cell. He remembered having been told in the Army Officer's School, that nudism was against all forms of government and probably the most anarchic act a man could do was to get his clothes off. This thought frequently assailed him before making love and was the reason for the extensive collection of pajamas and bathrobes, all khaki of course, he kept in the house of his mistress. How could anyone tell the difference between a colonel or a private, if all the clothes were off. In the battle field there would be chaos if a man had nothing to wear but his hide. Looking at the guard, he knew better. He could have dressed this pitiful figure in the brightest of all uniforms with golden braids and stars and still they would be certain of his rank.

The colonel thought, if the guard would give him the uniform, like a valet, it would be a victory. The voice of the guard became more imperative as he said again, "Sir, it is time..." Without a word the colonel walked towards the wooden box and began the mechanical gestures of putting his pants on. He detested the thought oozing from all his body that this was the last time he would ever put his pants on. He had not noticed until then, that action like many other usually insignificant actions would also become like landmarks for him, and only for him , just because they were being done for the last time.

With the uniform against his skin, the colonel again felt protected and almost invincible. He followed the guard into the hall and encountered to his surprise a small group of civilians. The secretary of the tribunal was among them. They all seemed to be anxious and by their appearance seemed also to be very unimportant. Without speaking the guard efficiently handcuffed the colonel. Suspecting that this was the beginning of the ritual of his execution, he asked "Who is in charge?" Nobody was. Impatiently, began to walk toward the door leading to the park where the firing squad were supposed to be stationed. "No, sir, this way please." He followed. After a brief walk, the group entered a large and well lit room. In the center, there was a large desk. In one corner, a cot, covered with a dark olive blanket. Sitting on it was a short man with a beard and a black beret with a silver star in it. The colonel soon recognized this man as the second-in-command of the revolutionary movement. This mysterious fighter had defeated most of the choicest regular army troops throughout the island. Whoever fought against him learned to respect his cunning and determination. The colonel was surprised to find how short and slight his body was. And how feminine the lips were. Without standing the man said "---what a pity it will be." "What a pity it will be," he repeated, "when they shoot you." And then after a pause: "There is still time for you to do some good. For the motherland. For yourself. For your wife. Repent, admit to your mistakes". He continued to speak but without conviction. The colonel began to feel bored again. The black beret stood up. The colonel thought "How short he is, how very short he is." The colonel began to smile. Soon, he began to laugh. As his body convulsed with laughter, the nearby figure began to curl. He shriveled down to the cot and screamed,

"Take him away. Now." Aware of their failure, the group took the colonel back to the cell.

It was dark. It was very warm and he began to perspire. The noises coming towards him in little waves revealed that a large crowd was gathering. The awareness of the necessity of facing the public again, slowed down his movements. My public, he thought, with the pride of a veteran actor. Most of them have been faithful. They were present during the arrest. They followed him to the original detention quarters. They waited in long lines for a seat in the courtroom. And now, by special permission, some privileged ones would see all stages of the grand finale. The others, would have to accept witnessing the execution from a distance or from television sets. Yes, even that had been scheduled. His execution would be transmitted throughout the entire island, so people would live with the awareness that it takes time for the justice of the Revolution to reach the culprits, but once having done so, it executes them. While he was trying to button his shirt, a small black speck on his chest attracted his attention. He had for many years, since his adolescence, many birthmarks, but this one was new. He stared at it. Then lifted the dark speck with his fingernail and examined it closely. When it began to move, he knew the truth. A vaguely familiar latin name came almost automatically to his lips: "Pediculus corporis." Body lice. In the Officer's Academy, the young cadets had been taught how to exterminate these insects which would tend to appear in crowds at times of a catastrophe. To his mind came the olive green booklet on Military Rules and Regulations for the Control of Communicable Disease issued by the Army. He mentally unfolded pages and pages in search for one page. Ah, he thought, page 67 under capital 'D' and with the title of *General Measures*, he read, through the heavy dust of twenty years: "Section 1. Improvement of living conditions, with adequate provision for frequent bathing and washing of clothes. Section 2. Dusting of population with insecticide at proper intervals where they live under conditions favoring lousiness. Section 3. Immunization may be offered to an entire population." Section 3 stuck in his mind like the dragging end of a damaged phonographic record. "Immunization may be offered to an entire population." "May be offered to an entire population." "To an entire population." The words seemed to have a powerful attraction for the moment, far more than the thought of what was about to happen. The latter stood quietly in a corner of his mind like a big, yet tame, cat. Perhaps, he thought, the revolution was offering an immunization against a future epidemic. He had read in his school years, Huxley's *Brave New World* and Orwell's *1984*. He also knew that healthy bodies do not have ulcers just as healthy countries do not have revolutions. With one exception, he thought. Immunization. It is then and only then that a healthy body can harbor an ulcer. For awhile. But, it is during that time that the body can be assailed with fever. And, it is during that time that a part of that body can die. Or suffer. But that suffering is necessary to prevent greater ills. He remembered having used his soldiers to enforce vaccinations and immunizations. He had for a moment a feeling of ease, a semblance of peace because perhaps he now knew why it was that he was going to die.

His bliss was interrupted by two voices. One in his mind and the other in the cell, outside of himself. One saying, "Sir, you are cracking up" and the other "Sir, it is time." He felt like a god in the cool night, bathed in the moonlight. He perceived himself as if drunk with a generous wine. There was a brief moment of confusion. That night, the heroes, the brave efficient leaders of the Revolution were going to execute eight men, but they brought only seven coffins. Made with haste. With the nails, black and rusty sticking out in the side planks of cheap pine. Yet, only seven. And eight men were to die. It would take one or two hours to bring the extra coffin from the other side of town, where the warehouse was. And nobody wanted to wait. The colonel checked his pockets. He still had eight cigarettes. He could wait. Soberly, he told them so. He stood there and watched the repetition of the same scene. Until all the prisoners to be executed lay in a bloody pile close to the wall. After a wait of three cigarettes, his coffin arrived. It was then announced that there would not be any further delays. He began to walk toward the wall. The terrain was uneven. And dark. He misstepped into a deep hole in the ground and fell. Rapidly, he stood up. He approached the wall. Nobody dared to mention a blind-fold. He stood in a martial attitude. The officer in charge gave the initial order: "Prepare arms." And then: "Aim." The colonel, without changing the posture of his head, looked at his dirty shoes once more.

Something annoyed him. During his fall, he had undone the cuff of his trousers on the right leg. He raised both arms as if pleading for time. The officer, hopeful that perhaps a word or two of repentance, or guilt, or even fear would come from the colonel's tight lips, gave the order: "Hold." The expectation was written in every face and in every twitch of the bodies of the execution squad. The colonel knelt slowly. At last, they all thought, at last. He may even ask for time. For forgiveness. With precise movements of both hands, the colonel straightened his cuff neatly. He stood up again and with a defiant smile on his lips, under the poorly trimmed mustache, he yelled: "Now you may fire."

And they did.

The poem which follows, was found among the meager belongings left by the Colonel, in the otherwise empty wooden box in his cell.

Until the present day, friends and enemies of the Colonel still argue to whom he dedicated his final writing.

Was it to a woman...? Or was it to his country...?

MI AMOR POR TÍ NO MORIRÁ CONMIGO, VIVIRÁ SIEMPRE

Mi amor por tí, no morirá conmigo
se quedará dormido, junto a tus ojos claros
y te dirá como yo no he podido
todas las angustias de mi amor frustrado.

Besará con ternura tus negros cabellos
susurrará a tus oído palabras de amor
y te dará en los labios, todos esos besos
que ahora laten en mi pobre corazón.

Caminará a tu lado como eterno compañero
mudo y adolorido espectro, ignorado por tí
y cuando te estremezcas al sentir su aliento
te sentirás sola y triste y pensarás en mí.

Solo cuando tu cuerpo y el mío seran sombras
lívida y opacas cansadas de vivir
es que este amor mío, que ahora solo te nombra
poseerá tu alma y será feliz.

Y es por eso que te clavo en mi mente
y que en mis noches de insomnio te sigo
porque mi amor por tí, no morirá conmigo
vivirá siempre, siempre, siempre...
                                junto a tí,
                                      mujer.

Mi amor por tí, no morirá conmigo vivirá
Siempre.-

Mi amor por tí, no morirá conmigo
se quedará dormido, junto a tus ojos claros
y te dirá como yo no he podido
todas las angustias de mi amor frustrado.

Besará con ternura tus negros cabellos
susurrará a tu oído palabras de amor
y te dará en los labios, todos esos besos
que ahora solo laten en mi pobre corazón.

Caminará a tu lado como eterno compañero
mudo y adolorido espectro, ignorado por tí
y cuando te estremezcas al sentir su aliento
te sentirás sola y triste y pensarás en mí.

Solo cuando tu cuerpo y el mío sean sombras
lívidas y opacas cansadas de vivir
es que este amor mío, que ahora solo te nombra
poseerá tu alma y será feliz.

Y es por eso que te clavo en mi mente
y que en mis noches de insomnio te sigo
porque mi amor por tí; no morirá conmigo
vivirá siempre, siempre, siempre........
                    Junto a tí
                        mujer.

FACES WITHOUT A STORY

A note regarding these photographs:
   The photographic material presented herein has had a long and dangerous journey out of Cuba into your hands. Thus, we hope that you will accept the imperfections that have occurred as the consequence of their arduous trip.

At the Presidential Palace,
Havana, Cuba.
Last days of 1958.

– Section A –

At the Cuban Army National Headquarters.
Camp Columbia,
Havana, Cuba.
January 1, 1959.

– Section B –

CONFECCIONADO POR LA SECCION DE INGENIERIA
DEL ESTADO MAYOR GENERAL DEL EJERCITO

Aboard Cuban Military Aircraft,
January 1, 1959.

– Section C –

At Moncada Army Barracks,
Santiago de Cuba, Cuba.
January 1, 1959.

– Section D –

26 JUL

At the Airport.
City and Province of Camagüey.
Early evening, January 3, 1959.

– Section E –

At the Airport.
City and Province of Camagüey.
Late evening, January 3, 1959.

– Section F –

The Shark in the Dining Room,
with his Prey.

– Section G –

Farm "La Malanga,"
in Ceiba Mocha, Matanzas, Cuba.
January 5, 1959.

– Section H –

A RETROSPECTIVE LOOK AT GORGONS, HYDRAS & CHIMERAS

Photo Section A:

39: The President of the Republic of Cuba, Fulgencio Batista y Zaldívar, during a press conference, smiles with satisfaction. In the center, in a white uniform, is his closest friend and top military assistant who, after escaping Cuba, committed suicide in Caracas, Venezuela in 1975. To the extreme left, is the indistinct figure of Doctor Casto Mier Zurbano, attorney, journalist and politician, who will play a significant role in the story that unfolds throughout the graphic evidence.

The question of why it is that Batista, the supreme ruler of the Island of Cuba, decided to leave abruptly in the early morning of January 1st, 1959 (leaving behind a posh New Year Eve Party) has never been completely answered. The truth is rather simple. Although it has been assumed that he did so because of the strength of Fidel Castro's forces, this is not entirely true. The so-called Rebel Army consisted of a few hundred soldiers, poorly armed and fed, mostly concentrated in a mountainous terrain known as "La Sierra Maestra," located in the extreme eastern portion of the island. This region in the Oriente Province was geographically far removed from Havana. The rebel underground movement was represented by a handful of brave and poorly organized group of terrorists in the urban areas. Batista was a man who had in his life only one main passion. He did not smoke, although he would enjoy a cigar on rare occasions, did not drink alcohol, and was not a gambler. His main interest in life, other than politics and military life, was romantic involvement with women. He was, in the last days of his control of the island, extremely distressed by the effects on his love life by the security measures adopted by his Secret Police. At times, if he had any romantic plans, these would be either changed or cancelled completely. His initial thrills of making love to a woman in a room crowded by several of his trusted men armed with machine guns, soon vanished. His hopes and dreams were that he could resign, leave Cuba and move to his exclusive mansion in Daytona Beach, Florida, where he could lead a life of enjoyment. He also expected forgiveness and benign neglect from the people that he was leaving behind.

All of Batista's plans were founded into what was known of Fidel Castro Ruz, at the time of this press conference. His knowledge was derived from historical facts corroborated by reports from his efficient Service of Military Intelligence. Fidel appeared to be a mass of contradictions. He was a man of intense emotions and fierce hates. He was, or professed to be anti-communist but was himself a Socialist. He hated intellectuals, but had obtained a doctorate degree from the University of Havana. He often talked about his distrust of lying and cruelty in life, but was proud of his ferocity. Also, his trail of killings extended from the city of Havana, through Bogotá, Colombia, ending in Santiago de Cuba, in the assault to the Army Post Moncada, where even the soldiers in the army hospital were shot in their beds. Fidel would write in letter to a close friend of Casto Mier describing the action of the morning of July 26, 1953: "History has never witnessed such a bloody massacre!" Thus, Batista thought that Fidel, as most psychopathic homicidal personalities, would have trouble becoming a successful leader. It appeared that Fidel had been able to survive only because he had lived on the fringes of society, and was constantly on the move. And that like other similar delinquents his downfall was somehow inevitable.

A factor hardly ever mentioned, which according to some, would have a profound influence in the outcome of the historic struggle between these men was the race and religion of Batista and Fidel Castro. Batista was a mulatto of humble origins whereas Castro was a white man the son of wealthy landowners of Spanish descent. Both were overtly catholics; Fidel received and extensive education at a Jesuit school. Yet there were reports in general circulation that both of them were members of a popular cult, akin to voo-doo, termed brujería. This cult of West African origin is a primitive religion based on the belief in sorcery and operates through the power of fetishes, potions, blood sacrifices and complex rituals. The colors of the flag of the Revolution of Fidel Castro, black and red, correspond to one of the most important gods of the African Pantheon. This african god named Elegguá happens to be "The Doorman". Whether this god, also called in his most sinister aspects, Eshú, opened the door to Fidel as he was closing the door to Batista on the early morning of January 1, 1959, is not known.

Photo Section B:

41: Casto Mier greets Colonel Ramón Barquín on his arrival to the Military Camp of Columbia. The colonel has just been released from prison and still is wearing the uniform pants of the Isle of Pine Penitentiary. He was imprisoned because of an attempt to overthrow Batista out of the Government and was the leader of a movement named the 'Conspiracy of the Pure". The term was applied because the officers involved were that portion of the military forces considered to be free of corruption. In absence of any other higher ranked officer he took command of the Military Camp. It is said in jest when it was announced that President Batista fled the island his generals did not ask , "Where are my troops?" or "Where is my gun?" but rather, "Where is my plane?." They all escaped in their personal aircraft.

The offices in the background are those of the Joint Chief of Staff (Cuartel Cabo Parrado) at the Cuban Army National Headquarters.

42: Colonel Barquín and Casto Mier greet jubilant members of the underground just arriving at the Columbia Military Camp after the news that Batista and his generals have left Cuba.

43: Colonel Barquín makes multiple attempts to reach by telephone the forces of the rebel army and talk to Comandante Fidel Castro. They were all unsuccessful. A decision was reached to have Casto Mier take to Fidel Castro a formal proposal for the creation of a Joint Ruling Commission to govern Cuba.

44: Casto Mier greets the first rebel soldier who entered the Columbia Military Camp. To the left of Casto Mier is an officer of the Cuban National Army. It is noteworthy that there is no animosity between the two soldiers. The prevailing notion was that once Batista and his generals departed, a climate of harmony would soon prevail among all Cubans.

45: The first rebel soldier to enter Camp Columbia is welcomed at the offices of the Cuban Army National Headquarters by Colonel Barquín.

46: The jubilant mood is prevalent. Colonel Barquin and a rebel officer pause to light cigars and share some recent experiences.

47: In the center and with a military officer cap is Colonel Angel Villafaña. He had been released from the Penitentiary of Isle of Pine a few hours before. Like Colonel Barquín he was imprisoned after an attempt to overthrow the government of Batista. He took command of the Cuban Air Force but accepted Colonel Barquín as Chief of the Cuban National Army.

48: A group of members of the Cuban National Army with Colonel Angel Villafaña, recently appointed Chief of the Cuban Air Force. He is at center of the picture with military cap and a cigar in his left hand.

49: Comandante Aldo Vera with other members of the underground. They all display the weapons used in their daily struggle against the government of Batista. Note the hand grenade in one member's belt. They came to Columbia Camp to place themselves under the command of Colonel Barquín. With the passage of time they left Cuba in disgrace. Vera died in Puerto Rico following a mysterious terrorist attack. His friends had all been killed in the City of Miami also on suspicious circumstances.

50:   Immediately adjacent to Casto Mier is General Jorge García Tuñon. He came to Camp Columbia hoping to become a part of the Government proposed by Colonel Barquín. This general had been a member of the "Conspiracy of the Pure." He escaped imprisonment and was exiled in Miami. After the General was a few days in Havana, and when Fidel Castro knew he was in Columbia Camp, it was ordered that he be arrested. He had little choice but to escape to Miami again.

In summary, Batista left Cuba voluntarily in the early morning of the first of January of 1959, accompanied by his family, friends and very high ranking military officers. Upon the news of his departure, certain military men who had been unsuccessful in a revolution against Batista were released from prison and flown in military aircraft into Camp Columbia, Headquarters of the Cuban National Army. Colonel Barquín who assumed the position of Chief of the Cuban National Army entrusted Casto Mier with the mission of taking to Fidel Castro a pact for the establishment of a Joint Commission. Documents to this effect were given to Casto Mier. Plans were completed for an immediate departure to Santiago de Cuba in the eastern portion of the island where the rebel forces were located.

Photo Section C:

52: Casto Mier with a group of newspaper reporters aboard a Cuban Air Force C-47 on his way to Santiago de Cuba in Oriente Province where the rebel army was stationed.

His mission: To carry documents from Colonel Ramón Barquín, Acting Chief of the Cuban National Army to Comandante Fidel Castro, proposing a truce and the formation of a Joint Commission for the ruling of Cuba.

Photo Section D:

54:   Upon arrival at Santiago de Cuba, capital city of Oriente province, Casto Mier as deputy of Colonel Barquín seeks contact with the civilian representatives of the rebel forces. The first person that he reached was Manuel Urrutia Lleo. He had been designated by Fidel Castro as President of Cuba. In addition, he received authorization to form a cabinet and begin the organization of the new government with its center in Santiago de Cuba. He appears in the center listening to Casto Mier, who states his intention to discuss political matters with Fidel Castro. At the time of this meeting, Fidel Castro was mobilizing the rebel forces to begin a march in a westerly direction towards Havana. Thus, Casto Mier would not be able to meet with Fidel in Santiago de Cuba.

55:   Two prominent members of the of the rebel forces. To the left is Dr. Faustino Pérez, who was with Fidel Castro in the Sierra Maestra, the highest mountain in Cuba and an ideal place of refuge for the Revolutionary forces. Armando Hart, to the right, had been released from prison. Initially, briefly in Camp Columbia, he decided to fly immediately to Santiago de Cuba and reach the newly nominated President of Cuba, Manuel Urrutia Lleo. Faustino Pérez was a physician; Hart, an attorney.

56:   To the extreme right is Colonel Jose Rego Rubido, who listens to an emotional speech given by Comandante Raúl Castro Ruz, brother of Fidel. The Colonel Rego Rubido was in command of the Moncada Army Camp, the largest stronghold of the Cuban National Army in Santiago de Cuba. He surrendered to Raúl Castro. The man on the extreme left, with a beard and a hand grenade on the left side of the chest, is Comandante Huberto Matos. This devoted Rebel Army officer was named Chief of the Rebel Forces of the Province of Camagüey. Ultimately, he was accused of conspiring against Fidel Castro, tried and condemned to twenty years in prison. In the lower right corner of the photograph appears the signature of Raúl Castro.

57: Casto Mier begins to reveal to Raúl Castro the nature of the mission given to him by Colonel Ramón Barquín, in the presence of Colonel Rego Rubido.

58: Further exposition of the possible pact between the Rebel Army and the Cuban National Army brings an enigmatic expression to the face of Comandante Raúl Castro, whereas a smile appears on the lips of Colonel Rego Rubido.

59: Raúl Castro, enjoying a pipe and surrounded by his officers, reads the document presented to him by Casto Mier. Rumors and legends about Raúl Castro abound but he has remained the most mysterious individual of the Revolution.

60: Comandante Fidel Castro Ruz addressing an audience of soldiers prior to his departure and slow march toward Havana. Next stop, the city of Camagüey, where an historic meeting with Casto Mier awaits.

PHOTO SECTION E:

62: Casto Mier with a group of selected high ranking officers of the Rebel Army. The lady is Celia Sanchez Manduley, lover of Fidel Castro. Years later she will die of cancer. At this time Casto Mier, unable to reach Fidel Castro in person, has discussed the details of the proposed peace agreement only with Raúl Castro Ruz.

63: Fidel Castro surrounded by the high command of the Rebel Army. In addition, some of the members of the Cuban Army Air Force join the group. The latter belong to the tactical group in control of the Military Aircraft of the island. The man with the white hat to the extreme left of the picture is Comandante Calixto García. Next to him, with a black beret displaying a fierce expression, is Comandante Augusto Martínez Sánchez, who later on became a minister in the initial cabinet of Fidel Castro. To the back of and behind the black rebel soldier is Comandante Víctor Borbón. In the center is Fidel Castro Ruz. The second man from the right, with a white hat, beard and multiple devotional medals seen through his open shirt, is Comandante Víctor Mora. He displays a hand grenade hanging from his belt; a common practice among high ranking members of the Rebel Army. Víctor Mora was initially designated Chief of the Rebel Army in the province of Camagüey, to be replaced later on by Huberto Matos.

64: It had happened at last. Casto Mier is able to present to Comandante Fidel Castro, leader of the Rebel Army, the proposal of Colonel Ramón Barquín, provisional Chief of the Cuban National Army. The pact aims to achieve a peaceful agreement between the two armies and thereby spare the island of Cuba from the expected mass slaughter. Fidel Castro quickly answers that he is not interested in any change from his original plans. He states that the bloody process to come is inevitable. He adds that the Cuban population will recover rapidly and effectively, and that normal lives with much happiness will be possible.

65: An intense discussion between Casto Mier and Fidel Castro, who repeats the statement that he has his own intentions and is unwilling to have any kind of truce with any member of the Cuban National Army.

66: Fidel Castro proceeds to write his definitive answer in a document.

67-68-69: Casto Mier makes repeated attempts to convince Fidel Castro that no agreement between the two armies will result in further blood loss and resulting deep division of the Cuban population. On page 69 the discussion becomes rather inflamed. Fidel has at this time only one aim, he says. And that aim is power.

In summary, the mission of Casto Mier is a complete failure. The Castro brothers and officers of the Rebel Army, exultant in their victory, fail to see that the upcoming revolutionary blood bath will result in continual warfare and bleak prosperity for Cuba.

Photo Section F:

71: Fidel Castro, during a speech directed to the Cuban Army Air Force personnel who still remain in control of military aircraft. He is pouring forth a tale of triumph and glory for those who will help him bring the war within close distance of its end. It is quite impossible to capture the sense of his words but a careful scrutiny of his face reveals the nature of his promise. All efforts are directed to convince the pilots to surrender.

72: Fidel Castro in a mellow mood continues to plead with the Cuban Army pilots.

73, 74, 75: During the conversation with the Cuban Army pilots, Fidel Castro lights a cigar and smokes it, in his characteristic manner. Displayed on his left wrist are the famous two wrist watches which he always wore during combat.

76: Out of the barracks, Fidel Castro again repeats to Casto Mier his determination to proceed with his own personal plans without accepting the offer of Colonel Barquín.

PHOTO SECTION G:

78: Fidel Castro Ruz, surrounded by his initial victims. These pilots, members of the Cuban Army Air Force, finally surrendered, trusting the reassuring words of Fidel. They were immediately placed in prison. They were court-martialled and found innocent. When Fidel Castro was informed of the Court decision he annulled the not-guilty sentence and ordered a second trial. This time, all the pilots were condemned to thirty years in prison. The President of the Court of the initial trial, Comandante Pena, committed suicide when he heard of the second trial.

The justice of the Revolution became emboldened by the public's acceptance of such severe sentences. In Cuba , prior to Fidel, there was no death penalty. The creation of such sentences, coupled with its application on a retroactive fashion, allowed the new Cuban government to carry out a great number of executions in the first few days of January, 1959. The words "To the Wall" ("Al Paredón") became a popular cry of the masses. The prisoners, members of the former Cuban military, were often executed in public. In several instances the executions were televised to the whole island. Although condemned to die "at dawn" many executions were delayed until noon, waiting for lighting conditions which would permit a more accurate rendition of the spectacle. The public was encouraged to attend the public executions. Such attendance, the Rebel Government thought, made each citizen an accomplice to the murder. It was not uncommon to see a Cuban mother propping up a child above her head so the toddler could see the final discharge of the firing squad rifles into the body of the victim.

Photo Section H:

80: The farm where Casto Mier Zurbano retired at the end of his unsuccessful mission to meditate, as he read the *Discourses* of Epictetus. In "Book One", the Greek stoic philosopher ponders "Of the Things which are and the Things which are not in our power." In the weeks that followed he would defend many officers of the Cuban Army, loyal to Batista. All of these men, except one, were executed.

Casto Mier, as he was well known, was a Cuban writer, lawyer and astute politician. He was born in Matanzas in 1906, educated in the city of his birth, moved to Havana to work in one of the earliest radio stations, the CMQ. He was essentially a political writer, but to earn his living practiced corporate law and was deeply involved in national politics. He died in Miami with the conviction that the triumph of Fidel Castro and his sustained survival was due to the inadequacy of the Cuban people to cope with the demand of their destiny.